SUNSET LEGACY

- Memories of a Life Well Lived -

by

Edward M. Prescott

PublishAmerica
Baltimore

ISBN: 1-60610-547-7
PUBLISHED BY PUBLISHAMERICA, LLLP
www.publishamerica.com
Baltimore

Printed in the United States of America

FOREWORD

The thoughts expressed herein and the words used to express them came from within the depth of my being. Each poem or writing expressed my innermost thoughts about the particular subject. The inspiration came, in many cases, from exterior stimulation, such as beautiful places: The Old Church On Braintree Hill - June 4, 1981, The Silent Sentinel - November 1989, and My Kids - December 1990.

The poem should have been titled OUR KIDS to memorialize their mother, whom God called home at the early age of forty-seven years. They were ours, and never will be just mine. The emotion of the moment clouded my thinking and I thoughtlessly claimed them "mine" not "ours".

I dedicate these works to the memory of my first wife, Paula, and to our children, Paul, Mark, John and Terri; and to my present wife, Mary Anne. Mary Anne is a source of love, support and inspiration, for which I am eternally grateful.

May the works contained herein be a source of pleasure and inspiration.

TABLE OF CONTENTS

THE OLD CHURCH ON BRAINTREE HILL

The pulpit stands empty,
The bell from its tower long gone.
There is no thundering organ,
No grand hymn singing choir.

No congregation arrives on Sunday morning,
The rows of pews to fill.
But there lingers His ever-present spirit
In the old church on Braintree Hill.

In the church's shadow lies its cemetery
Surrounded by a white wooden fence.
The bodies of the faithful rest here,
Their souls with God in Heaven.

The monuments, short stories tell.
Life's history set in stone.
For some on earth a living hell,
Now with God in joy and peace.

The early morning sun dries up the dew,
The grass in bright green and flowers in bloom.
Sunlight reflects from monuments.
Some very old, some quite new.

Within this lovely place there is no grief,
No sorrow, no despair, no hatred, no testing of will.
God's holy spirit lingers, watching over the faithful
Eternally resting beside the old church on Braintree Hill.

June 4, 1981

THE SILENT SENTINEL

There he stands on the village green,
In summer's heat and winter's cold blast.
He reminds us of what is unseen,
A bloody war fought in the dim past.

Does he look like someone we know?
Was it the young man next door
Who was full of life's youthful glow,
Now gone from earth forevermore?

He looks out through unseeing eyes,
Standing there straight and tall.
He never heard the battle cries,
On no deadly field did he fall.

He counts not the town clock's chimes,
He notes not the hours going swiftly by.
He reminds us of past times,
A gray stone soldier under a blue sky.

He is a symbol of national pride,
Part of each town's treasure.
A memorial to those who died;
A sacrifice that's hard to measure.

He is each one who made it through,
Standing there so straight and tall.
He is the symbol of a nation new -
A land free and united for all.

November 1981

MY KIDS

As I sit in my recliner,
I clearly see them all.
They are a constant reminder,
My kid's pictures on the wall.

Some serious, some a smile,
I look with love at one and all.
They were with us so short a while,
Now there's often a short phone call.

As I study them, what are they thinking?
Do they remember their young carefree days?
Do they wonder "Is Dad's time here shrinking?"
They are a blessing in so many ways.

As I sit here studying them all,
I also see their mother,
The fairest and loveliest of all,
Giving freely her love to one, than another.

What stories these pictures tell,
A big part of our past happy life.
God's love and care treated me well,
Four lovely kids and a wonderful wife.

January 1989

BROOKFIELD AT CHRISTMAS

A small village on a hill
Overlooking a pretty valley,
A small lake and floating bridge.
A special creation of God's will.

Christmas, a lovely time of year,
Snow-covered fields reflect moonlight.
Decorated trees light up the night,
The Christ Child's coming is near.

Tonight we gather here to sing,
To lift our voices in praise.
Silent Night, Hark The Herald Angels Sing.
Welcome to Brookfield, Holy King!

For you we give thanks,
Joy to the world, this holy season!
Watch over us and guide us, we pray,
As we celebrate your coming birthday.

December 21, 1989

HARVEST MOON

Shine on, harvest moon
Floating along on high.
Winter is coming soon,
Light up the evening sky.

Cast down your golden glow,
Over ripe crops standing below
Gently reflect the night time frost,
A reminder of summertime lost.

Your flight signs a changing season
From summers warmth to autumn's chill.
It is not for us to question or reason,
Just one more sign of God's will.

Soon it will be winter, long and cold.
Jack Frost will reign supreme.
The earth will be covered with farmer's gold,
Winter clamps an icy grip on field and stream.

Through it all, we slip, slide and stumble,
Looking eagerly for signs of Spring.
Awaiting lightning's flash and thunder's rumble
And Migrating birds on the wing.

September 1982

EACH DAY'S NEW DAWN

Wait not to enjoy life's abundant pleasure,
Such moments slip by and are swiftly gone.
Memories provide old age's richest treasure;
Look at the sunset but await each day's new dawn.

Swiftly flows and ebbs the tide of life,
As we journey across life's rough, rumbling sea.
Like a small boat tosses about, broken by strife,
Sailing on our final journey, into eternity.

Record in the log of life each day
The happiness given to others.
Be generous with good words, actions and deeds.
Extend the hand of fellowship to all,
As sisters and brothers.
Allow not your garden of life
To grow bitterness weeds.

Seek each day that elusive goal, "Peace of Mind",
Worry not about mistakes of yesterday, that's done.
Seek love, joy and happiness, a rare valuable find.
Be happy and productive from rising to setting sun.

JENNA

Jenna, a beautiful baby girl,
Now all of one year old.
Prettier than a valuable pearl,
A smile lovelier than gold.

Jenna likes to run and play,
She is active and excited.
Her antics make our day,
Watching her play, we are delighted.

Jenna, the star of family pride,
She is the center of attention.
She loves a horsy-back ride,
A ride with no destination.

Jenna is busy as a bee,
Marching from place to place.
Suddenly she is at your knee
A lovely smile on a pretty face.

October 27, 2006

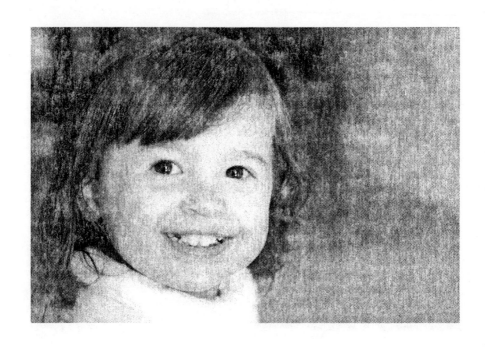

KYLIE ELIZABETH

Kylie, a smiling happy child at play.
A beautiful brown-eyed girl.
Hair with lots of natural curl,
Her smile would steal your heart away.

While playing she's busy as a bee,
First she is here and then she's there.
Where she is next, just wait and see.
She could be playing anywhere!

She loves her babies and her rabbit rag,
They give her comfort, she gives them love.
Her big sister, Jenna, is her hero but there
Are times when they give each other a shove.

Kylie is like the sunlight -
Cheerful, happy and bright.
She is like the morning sunrise
After a long dark night.

MR. WIND

He sweeps across the plains,
From where no one knows.
He brings clouds and the rains,
No one knows where he goes.

He makes fence wire whistle,
He sends leaves racing from place to place
He pulls seeds from the thistle,
He gently caresses Queen Anne's Lace.

He makes loose shutters chatter,
Unhooked doors swing to and fro -
His chill blast makes teeth chatter,
A very sure sign of snow.

At times he whistles a happy tune,
He keeps flying children's kites.
He is warm and gentle in June
In winter he stings and bites.

April 6, 2004

FUN IN THE RAIN

The clouds darkened,
Thunder rumbled and growled.
Soon it was raining cats and dogs,
The street was filled with mud poodles.

Children romped and stomped.
Giggles and laughter prevailed.
Through puddles they clomped.
Looking for more to be assailed.

The wetter, the better!
This was really fun!
Getting wetter and wetter,
Through the puddles they run.

Soon the fun comes to an end,
A loud shout from the door.
The fun was at an end.
Some bottoms would soon be sore.

THE MAGNET OF MUD

A temptation children cannot resist,
What a great looking play site!
Should we or should we not go?
What the heck! Let's go!

In we go, romping and stomping,
Mud and water splashing everywhere.
Muddy and wet, we don't care!
Not a thought of what's to come…

Soon the joy and laughter ceases,
A loud voice commands "COME HERE!"
We do, feeling a twinge of fear,
Hopefully it doesn't mean a sore rear.

"Look at you! What a Mess!
How will I ever get you clean?
Clothes off and into the bath,
Now dry off and into pajamas!
You surely must know what I mean!"

HONKING ALONG

It was a warm Spring afternoon,
The wind blowing easily to the north.
Summer would be coming soon,
Time for the geese to be coming forth.

You hear them before you see them,
Faint at first then loud and clear.
They honk their loud anthem,
Year after year, after year.

Comes the Fall, they head the other way.
They alert us to the changing seasons.
Groups grow larger each day,
Only they know the reasons.

February 2005

ONE RAINY DAY

Tap, tap, tap, rain on the roof.
Gurgle, gurgle, it comes out the spout.
Water covered windows show proof -
It is definitely raining out!

We laugh and play in puddles,
We care not about getting wet!
We kick and stomp, making bubbles,
We have not heard from our parents yet.

Suddenly from the porch comes a call,
"What are you doing out there?"
From here, Dad looks seven feet tall,
We are going to get it - but where?

Into the house we make our way,
Dad looks and shakes his head.
This is the end of play for today,
We are soon on our way to bed.

September 2004

THE STORM

Mother Nature is in a state of wild rage,
her unpleasant disposition has been aroused.
She will release the storm from its cage
up high in the mountains where it is housed.

Huge dumpling-like clouds she will gather,
the wild untamed winds she will call.
The clouds she will fill up with water,
then torrents of rain will soon fall.

She will loose the terrible lightning,
followed by the rumbling thunder.
The chains and flashes very frightening;
it causes us to stand still and wonder.

Soon she will loose the mighty wind,
the land cannot escape her wrath.
Nature's disturber, the mighty wind
leaves great wreckage in it's path.

Soon her intense fury will be spent,
the torrent and noise will subside.
Children wonder where the storm went,
We tell them back to the mountain-side.

A GOLFER'S DREAM

I went to bed quite early.
I had one thing on my mind.
I could see it happen clearly,
A golf shot of a special kind!

I dreamed of a Hole-In-One,
I sent the ball soaring -
I was blinded by the sun,
Was I or was I not, scoring?

I studied the far-away scene,
That tiny white ball I did not see.
No white ball lying on the green,
My thoughts raced, where could it be?

I approached the flag with tentative step,
Dare I hope that the ball was in the cup?
At the sight my heart leapt…
And then…I woke up!

January 2005

A PUTTER'S LAMENT

Why, oh why do I play this game?
A jinx controls the little white ball.
I seek not glory or fame,
Another putt fails to fall.

A good drive high and far,
They are few and far between.
My goal is to make par,
A hole in one is but a dream.

What, oh what, do I do wrong?
Why does my dream not come through?
A good drive is like a song,
That's something I like to do.

When I lay down to sleep,
I dream of a Hole-in-One.
A memory I'd like to keep,
A dream is not yet done.

A GOOD DAY OF FISHING

One day my wife and I went fishing,
We used our small blue boat.
Our hopes were high with wishing,
We wanted to stay afloat.

The water was quiet and still,
A nice warm sunny day.
We went fishing with a will,
We're going to catch a big one today.

Mother enjoyed catching perch.
I was looking for that big bass.
By the hour we continued the search,
Dropping our bait near the tall grass.

Suddenly my lure he struck,
The fight was on to the end.
My pole would hold out, with luck,
His great fight I do commend.

To take this great fighter's life, I could not.
Gently I placed him back into the water.
Slowly back and forth I moved him,
Suddenly a big splash and he was gone.

July 2006
Keeler Bay, Lake Champlain

MY WIFE TOOK ME SHOPPING

"Don't sit there and vegetate!
Let's go shopping!"
Off to the store at a fast rate,
Soon from shelf to shelf, no stopping!

Up one aisle and down another,
Moving slowly with stops and starts.
Ducking and dodging each other,
Sometimes bumping other carts.

Back and forth, aisle after aisle.
A can of this, a can of that -
Trying hard to keep a smile,
Checking closely the content of fat.

Old friends often meet,
Stop and visit for awhile.
Forgotten are sore, tired feet,
Reminiscing often triggers a smile.

Soon the cart is very full,
Filled right up to the top.
It is not easy to pull and
We are tired enough to drop.

A NEW DAY

The night had been dark and dreary,
Dawn crept slowly from the darkness.
The sun peaked over the horizon,
A new day was being born.

Daylight crept over the landscape,
Shadows small at first, began to spread.
Sunlight created a vast blanket over the land
It was the beginning of a new day.

The chill of the night turned warm,
Dew covered grass yielded its moisture.
The sun flew higher as the day wore on,
A perfect summer day!

All good things must end,
Heavy clouds darkened the sky.
Soon torrents of rain fell -
How can we explain the reason why?

AN ERA GONE BY

The music was great,
Songs came from the heart.
Songs of love, not hate -
A time from a world apart.

The music was not "crash-bang"!
The songs came from within.
The hall with harmony rang,
Soft and sweet, no loud din.

The Jitterbug was at its height,
The music was always great.
We used to dance through the night,
A good way to share a date.

Those days we should remember,
They came and went by so fast.
A memory lingers like burning embers,
A better part of young life past.

January 29, 2005

FREDRICKSBURG

Here they come as on parade,
what a grand and glorious sight!
Soon their bodies will litter the grade,
there will be many sad homes tonight.

Take cover back of the stone wall,
load the gun and just wait.
Keep handy your powder and ball,
be sure, aim well, shoot straight.

See them drop like sheaves of wheat,
O, those poor fellows so young and brave!
There they lie in rows so neat,
all they have is a lonely grave.

Bacl they go in total disarray,
surely the fight they will not renew!
They must know they lost the day.
What more could they do?

Stand ready, here they come again!
They know not to accept defeat.
They keep coming as their ranks grow thin,
they have lost again, they must retreat.

GETTYSBURG—THE OTHER SIDE

"General Mead!
Shall we stand fast or move back?
What deposition needs to be made?
I fear they will soon make an attack,
We see them massing over in the glade."

"Look yonder, the round tops
are not cover manned,
In the woods beyond, the enemy is massing.
Forward, 20th Maine! Up the hill, take a stand!
We must stop them from passing!"

"Stand fast, boys, give them the lead and steel,
If they get through, all is lost!"
They must be stopped and brought to heel,
No matter what the cost!"

"General, now they are at Culp's Hill,
They must not be allowed to gain the top.
Our men must resist them with a will,
Their advance we must stop."

"Stay low, boys, take cover, the shells are flying!
Be ready, soon they will be coming over -
Shoot well, aim low, let them do the dying!
Drop them row up row in the new clover!"
Suddenly all the guns fall silent,
Bugle calls and drum rolls across the field.

"Look sharp, boys, they are coming!
If you have need, kneel and pray!"
They are getting closer, some now running.
Pray to God you live to see another day."

General Stannard:
"See in their lines…a gap!
Rise up, boys, fire fast at will -
We have them, they are in a trap!
Now is the time, shoot to kill!"

They are stopped, they can not go on!
For them, a high water mark.
They are stopped, the attack is ended,
You can hear the song of a lark.

All they had to give, they expended.
They turn back, their spirits broken.
They will not forget this day at Gettysburg;
By those alive, silent prayers were spoken.

A FAMILY'S LAMENT

When called to serve, you went.
You did your duty very well,
Then came that terrible evening,
in battles intense fury you fell.

Our pillows are wet with tears.
No sleep, just lying awake till dawn.
You were with us for a few short years,
now suddenly you are gone.

The last sound of Taps fades away,
one last look into your grave.
This is a very sorrowful day,
you were so young and brave.

The painful memory lingers on.
For a family, there is no end.
Oh, how we miss you, son,
Our young pal and best friend.

PRIME OF LIFE

With love and respect we remember
Three young men in the prime of life.
The memory of them glows like hot ember;
Sacrificed to the Gods of war and strife.

Young and brave they went to battle,
The enemy struck them with all its might.
Cannon and machine gun in deadly rattle,
They died there in this deadly fight.

Now does it matter who won?
It does, to family and friend.
Yes, three families lost a son,
Loyal and faithful to the end.

Home at last to final rest,
Their bodies lie not far apart.
They gave their very best,
They live on in our heart.

In Memory Of:
Barny Zelinskis
Bud McGarvin
Theodore Barnhart

WHERE THEY REST

Veterans Cemetery - Randolph Center

How quick the grave plots fill
As the WW2 generation becomes history.
No open spots on the hill,
Brave deeds an untold story.

Young, fearless and full of fight,
Giving their all in some distant land.
With strong faith their cause was right,
Many died on beaches of sand.

"Bring them home" was the call,
Bury them here or in the family plot.
Respect is due, they gave their all,
To ignore them we should not.

Many lie in some foreign land,
To visit their grave the family can not.
They spilled their blood in the sand,
They gave so much more than they got.

January 2005

THE GREEN MOUNTAIN BOYS

Their truth is marching on!
It has lived through many ages,
The Green Mountain Boys of history.
Their fearless bravery fills many pages.

Year after year, the tradition stays alive,
Their fearless bravery still well known.
When the call comes, they are the first to go,
Their fearless action survives the ages.

Today their tradition lives on,
Whenever called to duty, they go.
Service to God and country, above all.
Their goal to keep the lamp of freedom aglow.

To be a Green Mountain Boy is a duty,
To love and protect family and honor.
Freedom and unity for one and all.
They stand ready for the call.

Today's Green Mountain Boys valor lives on.
Armed, trained and ready to go.
Duty to family, God and country utmost,
Always ready to deal with the e
We are about to be driven in.
Help us prevent such fate,
Send the Vermonters in!

Vermonters, forward on the double!

We must try to save the day!
Our command faces fire trouble,
The enemy must be held at bay.

Forward, boys, follow the flag!
Let's show them our true colors.
Keep in line, boys, don't lag;
Let them see real valor!

Well done, boys, you turned the tide,
It's over! The enemy is pulling back.
For your work, you should feel pride,
Bravery under fire you do not lack.

Often now we hear the call,
Even though our ranks are thin.
We are asked to give our all
When they say "Send the Vermonters i

May 6, 1993

VETERANS

Our ranks are growing thin,
We are warriors of the past.
We fought a good fight to win,
We struggle again to make it last.

There is, it seems, no end to deadly war.
Before it ends a new one starts -
Causing broken homes and broken hearts.
All this hostility leaves scarring marks.

The world is in constant turmoil,
War and death seems never to end.
The world gets rid of one dictator,
Another one is waiting 'round the bend.

We who survived know the cost,
We respect and honor those we lost.
Their memory burns like hot embers,
White lined crosses cause us to remember.

JOHNNY

The train was ready to leave,
hugs, kisses then a goodbye.
Concerned parents grieve,
"Our boy was too young to die."

On a deadly field he fell,
battle takes it's toll one by one.
He had answered the call,
his duty honorably done.

Johnny did not come marching home,
he lies over there in a grave.
He was killed far from home,
young, fearless and brave.

Our son, we will always remember,
sadly we miss his great smile.
Each day is seven December.
He was with us for so short a while.

War is hell to say the least.
When will it ever end?
When will it ever end?
It stalks the world as a hungry beast,
repeating again and again.

NIGHTTIME IN A FOXHOLE

Muzzle flashes lighted the night sky,
from the distance a dull boom.
Tonight how many men will die;
brave young soldiers facing doom.

Will they survive this horrible night,
could you blame them for feeling fear?
Daylight or dark, they continue the fight,
thoughts of home and loved ones near.

In darkness comes the call "Medic!"
That last attack took a grave toll.
The outcome you can almost predict,
more lives added to the Death Roll.

War is hell, to say the very least,
with homes and families torn apart.
War stalks the world as a hungry beast
and it causes many a broken heart.

Someday may there be peace,
should the world come together.
Conflict and hatred would cease,
then life for all would be better.

HATRED

The world is full of hatred,
Vicious malice is all around.
The more harm someone can do,
The more they work to compound.

Grief caused to other is their joy,
Hatred and dislike is their goal.
The more grief they can cause, the better.
The product of a demented soul.

We deal with these people through life,
Their display of hate and anger never ends.
They know not how to love or be loved,
They dwell in the dungeon of strife.

They are a blight to society,
Their evil ways create destruction.
To the problems they create,
There is no limit, their life is a waste.

ANGER

ANGER, can be like a poison in a person's system -
an ongoing poison - and some people
cannot be cured of it.
It can be very destructive if it lives in a
person's system and become s a weapon
in a relationship.

ANGER, the enemy of self-control.
It advertises the loss of self-control…
It produces many an unhappy home.

ANGER, is the trigger finger of many a broken home,
and deadly disputes.

ANGER, has pulled the trigger in many murders.

ANGER, can lead to physical as well as mental abuse -
a continued mental disorder and bodily illness.

ANGER, may strike when you least expect it.
used as a defense is as weak as no defense at all.

ANGER, is no solution to a lingering problem.

ANGER, the curse of mankind sweeps the earth as a plague.
it sweeps the nation,

It travels as a fire storm

spreading across the country like the wind

it travels as a fire out of control
- injury and death resulting.

Will it ever come to an end?

A VERMONT STATE TROOPER

To be a Vermont State Trooper is an honor,
A privilege not granted to all.
Within a state trooper must reside
A willingness to answer any call.

In fair weather and foul,
The duty must be done.
To protect and defend the goal,
To protect the rights of anyone.

There can be no favor, it is one and all.
Treatment of all must be honest and fair.
A willingness to respond to any call,
At any time, any place, anywhere.

Our oath is a promise to protect.
To protect life and property for all.
Our actions must be honest and correct,
There is no excuse for misconduct at all.

VERMONT STATE POLICE

The night was dark and dreary,
Not a star visible in the sky.
Trouble was in the making,
Tonight someone would surely die.

Always ready and on guard,
Our State Troopers are prepared.
Some tasks are easy, some are hard;
Devotion to public safety equally shared.

Be it bright sun or deep snow,
They willingly answer any call.
The call for help comes in, "They Go";
Be it summer, winter or fall.

Their devotion to duty is above all,
Their sworn oath is to serve.
They never fail to answer a call.
It takes courage, honesty and nerve.

To a trooper, his oath is sacred,
His oath demands he will serve well.
He is committed to uphold the law
And his future one cannot foretell.

Old Troopers never die,
They just patrol away...
Here today, gone tomorrow.

ABOVE AND BEYOND

You found him where he lay,
The icy torrent rushing over him.
Would he live to see another day?
That chance appeared very thin.

Hesitate? No, that couldn't be done!
You acted with great speed.
There was a chance for him - only one.
You saved someone in desperate need.

Without you, a life would be lost.
You did not think "What about ME?"
You did not consider the cost -
Danger for yourself you did not see.

To save others, you took an oath,
No matter who, where or when.
Death could have claimed you both,
To you it mattered not, then.

A more selfless act one cannot render,
Or perform a more heroic deed,
Than one's own safety to surrender,
To save someone in desperate need.

***

For Officer Barbara O'Neill,
Northfield Police Department
For a heroic rescue of a man
trapped in a wrecked car.

June 1990

FRIENDS

Mike and Ellie

Friends true and loyal you are,
We have shared a happy friendly past.
Friends always - be we never too far,
May it continue through life to last.

Friends in time of joy or great stress,
When needed you both were there.
Your loving support was always more, not less.
You showed all how much you care.

Friends as we shared life's troubles,
The problems and tribulations of growing kids.
Some causing tears, some bringing smiles,
Teaching them what's right and what God forbids.

Friends still on your special day,
May God's love and care be with you.
Go in peace on your chosen way.
Enjoy health and happiness in all you do.

JUDGE WOLCHICK

You came to us from afar,
One year you were to stay.
That swift-passing year is over
And now you are on your way.

Each morning with your cheery hello,
You won all our hearts.
Now thru sleet, rain and snow
You will travel to other parts.

The year was a very busy one
With lots of cases for you to hear.
You were tired when day was done
But always of good cheer.

That you will be missed is very true,
To all of us you are very dear.
Bluntly put, we will miss you!

Please stop to see us when you are near.

JOHN

Our friend John has retired.
No more long work days.
Better retired than fired,
Still keeps busy in so many ways.

John worked hard for many years.
He is devoted to his lovely wife.
They go forward with faith, not tears,
Are known for their love of life.

Dust off the golf clubs, John!
The test is about to begin.
At the first tee the pressure is on,
A good tee shot rates a grin!

To lose to John would be a pleasure.
For our time together has been short.
Time well spent and to treasure,
John always smiles, always a good sport.

This masterpiece is at the end,
I don't know what else to say.
I salute a very good friend -
I admire him in every way.

THIS OLD ROBE

This old robe has served me well,
It's been with me for quite a spell.
I've worn it in the heat
And when it was cold.
It makes you feel humble
And sometimes bold.
Some were meek and mild
And some would really blow
But we took it all in stride,
Because in our job we took real pride.
Now as retirement time is near,
It's time for me - and this old robe -
To call it a career.

**Written for, dedicated to and read for him
At his retirement party on October 18, 1985.
John Connarn, a dedicated man with long
And dedicated service to the State of Vermont.**

THE CHILDREN ARE THE PAWNS

Anger and emotion rise to unbelievable heights
The children are the pawns.

Abusive language, name calling, verbal fights
The children are the pawns.

We say we love our children, they are the best.
The children are the pawns.

But we forget all except who wins the test.
The children are the pawns.

I'll keep those kids no matter what!
The children are the pawns.

No matter how deeply the injury may cut.
The children are the pawns.

You did me dirt, I'll never forget!
The children are the pawns.

Divorce, neither party want to bend.
The children are the pawns.

The parents fight on to a bitter end.
The children are the pawns.

58

IT'S MY FACE

It is mine, I was born with it.
It is to many, a mirror of my mind.

It reflects joy, sadness or wit.
It is private to me, one of a kind.

Like a hall of mirrors,
the reflection may be inaccurate.
My face is here, my thoughts
may be elsewhere.

Toward no man do I feel malice,
to no one do I wish harm or hurt.
My thoughts are mine, locked in a private place
What they may be, no man shuld subvert

My thoughts harm no one without action,
Their misunderstanding of my thoughts isn't fair.
No one should try to place me in mental inaction.
My face and my thoughts are mine

CLOUD FORMS

I sat studying the day-time sky,
Clouds of all shapes and forms.
Slowly they are drifting by,
Changing as they move along.

One is shaped like a huge fish,
One like a plate of mashed potatoes.
Another like a large submarine
In a large patch of blue like the ocean.

Patches of sky separates one from another,
A large dark cloud with sun-lighted edges,
A dark threatening one forecasts the rain.
Dark and threatening they drift overhead.
A blue and white masterpiece
Of shape, no sign of a storm.

A blue and white sky,
Not a sign of a storm.
A sight that triggers the imagination.
A special part of God's creation.

There is magic in a scene like this,
A magic blend of blue and white.
Shapes and sizes trigger the imagination -
A pleasant way to let your mind wander.

A BOWL OF CHERRIES

To some people life is like a bowl of cherries,
They think not about the pits inside.
They ignore the problems life carries,
It's easier to cast the thought of them aside.

To skip issues seems easier,
Just walk away and let it lie.
If you ignore it, it will go away,
It seems as easy as eating apple pie.

Ignoring problems does not make them go away,
It delays the final proper solution.
It's better to grin, bear it, and face it!
It clears the mind of long-term pollution.

Problems come and go -
To ignore them provides no solution,

Face it head-on and seek resolution.

SUCCESS

Success is an elusive goal for many,
Failure an everyday occurrence.
What should have gone right, went wrong.
How and why did it happen?

The very best of plans could fail.
Back off and make a fresh start!
Yield not to dismal failure,
Dig in and forge ahead.

There is a solution to most problems,
Giving up easily is not the way.
Stand your ground, then move ahead.
Success may be just a short step away.

Success is the end result of hard labor,
The end results of planning and thought.
Yield not to dismal failure,
Forge ahead and complete the task!

A WET DAY

The sky was dark and cloudy
Wind-blown trees waved back and forth.
A storm was on the way, no doubt,
Coming from the North.

No play outdoors today!

Rain drops rattled the rooftops,
Thick heavy clouds drifted along.
Not very nice for outdoor play,
The weatherman's forecast was wrong.

Rat-tat-tat - Rain on the roof!

Soon the house was full of action,
Toys were scattered everywhere.
Soon there were shouts and laughter,
"LET IT RAIN! WE DON'T CARE!"

After awhile the rainfall ends,
Clouds separate, the sun peeks through.
Now the scene of action changes -
Eyeing large puddles, we know what to do!

Stomp, stomp, splash, splash, splash!

Muddy water flying everywhere -

A sharp call comes from the house,

"You come in here, get out of there!"
Meekly as a mouse we go inside!

The reception there is not very warm,
We are about to face a different storm.
The result could be butt-side pain,
We were warned not to do that again."

WHEN WE WERE KIDS

The wind blew briskly from the North
Bare skin felt its time for bite.
A sure sign of winter coming forth,
It was a snowy night.

Soon snow on the ground was piling,
Blowing all about and drifting.
Young children watched, smiling,
Thoughts of good sledding uplifting.

Warmly dressed and ready for fun,
Get the old sled ready to go!
Happy thoughts of that first run,
Who will make the first track in the snow?

All too soon it's time for bed,
The end of a fun day -
For the night, park the old sled.
Tomorrow - more fun and play!

FEATHERED VISITORS

Tall trees stand in our backyard,
Sunlight on the trees case a shadow below.
This picture should be placed on a postcard,
The true beauty of winter to show.

Birds visit the seed filled feeders,
Their activity puts on a real good show.
They must be exceptional good readers,
They know the right place to go!

While here they fly too and fro -
From the nest to the feeder, then back they go.
They eat hungrily like it's their last meal,
They don't know it, but they have a real good deal.

WIND IN THE TREES

A strong wind danced across the valley,
Fallen leaves raced from place to place.
Leaves collected in the corner of an alley
As the wind continued its wild race.

Small limbs became barren as they thrashed about,
Stronger limbs shed their leaves more slowly.
At this pace leaves will be wildly scattered, no doubt,
Leaving the tree one looking barren and lowly.

When the wind died, the tree silently stood there.
All the leaves scattered and long gone -
Looking at the tree one limb held one leaf only,
The wind stopped at night, the last leaf fell at dawn.

Leaf barren limbs absorbed the morning sunlight,
Not a leaf-barren limb could be found -
Mother Nature had completed her duty,
Preparing the tree so snow could fall to the ground.

MOVIE OF NATURE

The weatherman predicted snow this morning.
At eight o'clock, his prediction came true.
Storm clouds had been forming overhead,
Slowly and lightly the snow came into view.

A new scene developed in our backyard,
With freshly fallen snow hugging the trees.
The earth soon had a covering white blanket,
Small squirrels scampered in the snowy breeze.

We have three squirrels in our backyard,
They race about and climb about in the trees.
They also regularly visit our hanging feeders.
Their antics are something to see and please.

There is one squirrel that is quite a clown,
He climbs atop of the feeder, then hangs down.
Our furry friend is Mother Nature's treasure
And should not be harmed in any way.

NO CALLING CARDS REQUIRED

Well-filled birdfeeders in our back yard,
Invitation to visit requires no calling card.
All they have to do is find their way to it
And enjoy the feast, including the suet.

Calling hours are not restricted,
Open hours are twenty-four hours a day.
Weather hours are not predicted,
All they have to do is know the way.

We do our best to keep the feeders filled.
They are placed for safe, easy visitation.
No harm or species requirement is willed,
Our guests find the treat a good situation!

REMEMBERING

Through many years I now look back,
At the time I was but a small boy.
I am now much older and I hope wiser.
Many past event memories bring me joy.

The experiences of life are many,
Success and failures included.
Winning at some, losing at others.
A time known as growing up.

To remember each event is impossible.
Some body scars are a strong reminder.
Family love lives on -
To me life couldn't have been kinder.

I have much to remember as I look back.
Each new day brings a new reminder,
With God's blessing I will stay on track
And life will continue to be kinder.

I WONDER

I wonder as I wander
Through life's rough, rumbling seas.
I wonder what lies out yonder,
What lies in store for me.

Each day brings new surprises,
I never know what to expect.
I am up and thinking as the sun rises,
I hope I do nothing I would regret.

To obtain the good life I strive,
To be a credit to one and all.
To live a long, useful life, I hope to survive.
I must continue my search and not fall.

As I look back over the many years,
Many of my goals have been achieved.
Past history releases many fears,
To look back over it all, I am relieved.

OVER THE YEARS

My name is Edward Prescott.

I'm five foot ten and a half inches in height
Since I was a young man I have always wanted to write.
It gives me great pleasure to take my pen in hand,
I do my very best to make poetry sound grand.

I am now eighty-one years of age,
It's a sincere pleasure to create page after page.
Through eighty-one years, I'm extremely blessed.
I find it exciting, something new to create.

Upon an exciting life I now look back.

In school when the whistle blew,
I wanted to score before I was through;
I was ready to get out and play the game,
I never sought after fortune or fame.

I am a survivor of a deadly war,
As I age, I think of it more and more.
Thank God we went in and did it right,
We put the belligerent enemy out of the fight.

When I returned home I became
A Vermont State Trooper, not quite the same
As anything I had ever done before -

I lasted twenty-four years and no more.

I've had a wonderful fulfilling life.

I'm now retired and enjoying married life
I am blessed with a lovely, devoted wife.
She is the sunlight for me every day -
I owe her a debt that I can not repay.

SUNSET LEGACY

As the years have passed and I grow older,
The winters have gotten longer and colder.
So I spend my days writing, to pass the time
And want to share with you my poetic rhyme.

I'd like to save my poems so you can remember
The thoughts and feelings I had in December.
The memories of a life that I lived well and free,
In these verses you will catch a glimpse of me.

Early Spring, I was just a young boy of ten
Who looked at life a bit differently then.
Summer came, and I tried out my wings,
I served my country proudly, all it brings.

Fall came, and I had become a young man
Looking after to my wife and family, best I can.
Times of laughter and later, times of tears -
A State Trooper I was for many years.

I tried to live a life that was upright and strong,
To teach my children what was right or wrong.
Now as I look back, how the time flew by -
I remember love with a tear-filled eye.

In later years, another family joined my own,
My wife had passed on, and I was so alone.
I needed the caring and support of Mary Ann,

Who brought beauty into my life once again.

Winter came when I really wasn't looking -
I sit back and smell something good cooking.
Each new day brings sunshine and hope to me,
As I write this - for you - my sunset legacy.

Dedicated to a forever friend,

NOT TO ME

The vehicle sped along the highway,
The speedometer read eighty-five.
It started to veer from side to side,
Crashing - and not a one left alive.

Four young kids died that night,
Their short young lives ended.
Good driving skills not on their side,
Careless driving can not be defended.

A trooper arrived on the scene,
A sight familiar to him or her.
Grieving parents have to be notified,
All too often these things occur.

Try as you will, you can't teach them.
All the answers they already know.
"It may have happened to him or her…